The Los Angeles City Guide

A Guidebook to Explore the Amazing City Of Los Angeles: Best Shops, Bars, Restaurant And Monument.

By

Easton Lincoln

damages, or monetary loss due to the information herein, either directly or indirectly.

Respective authors own all copyrights not held by the publisher.

The information herein is offered for informational purposes solely and is universal as so. The presentation of the information is without contract or any type of guarantee assurance.

The trademarks that are used are without any consent, and the publication of the trademark is without permission or backing by the trademark owner. All trademarks and brands within this book are for clarifying purposes only and are owned by the owners themselves, not affiliated with this document.

Contents

Introducing Los Angeles:

Los Angeles is the second-most populous city in the United States and is one of the largest in terms of land area. It is the hub of a five-county metro region and is seen as the pattern for the future metropolis—a city at the forefront of all the benefits and drawbacks of major cities. Los Angeles' reputation as a California paradise has been enhanced by the glitz of Hollywood, Beverly Hills, the Sunset Strip, & the world-famous beaches, which have all contributed to the city's extraordinary expansion. Los Angeles is a city of great diversity, with one of the largest Hispanic populations in the U.S., a significant Asian community, and significant communities of people from nearly every ethnic group on the planet. Los Angeles also is a major worldwide commercial and finance hub, as well as a manufacturing and tourism hub. In its huge aggregation of independent and quite diverse neighborhoods, the city has something for everyone: a sleek, ultra-modern center, miles of magnificent beaches, magnificent mansions and breathtaking canyon residences, and even some of the world's most luxurious shopping and restaurants. However, under the glitz is a struggling, racially divided city with extraordinarily high unemployment rates among young African Americans & Latinos.

Los Angeles, California! Few towns can claim to be so well-known over the world that they are solely known by their initials! L.A. draws tens of millions of people each year & is a must-see for anybody visiting California.

Every day, someone, somewhere, abandon everything in order to pursue his or her "American dream" of being famous and wealthy. Do not be surprised if you see a lot of want-to-be celebs at any time of day or night!

Chapter 1: Experience Los Angeles

Los Angeles is a truly wonderful city, with technicolor sunsets, an incomparably diversified eating scene, and a long history as the world's filmmaking capital.

Los Angeles is unlike any other metropolis on the planet. Every area pulsates with the energy of this bustling global metropolis; world-class performances, magnificent events, and breathtaking natural vistas await you at all hours of the day and night. Read on for unforgettable Los Angeles experiences, from the Historical Core in Downtown L.A. to a famed surf break in Malibu.

Here are some additional ways to immerse yourself in the enchantment of Los Angeles.

1.1 Visit the Venice Boardwalk to see the street performers

The worldwide famous Venice Ocean Front Walk (also known as "Boardwalk") is among the best sites in Los Angeles to watch people, from the colorful locals to tourists from all over the world. At the concrete boardwalk, there's something for everyone: restaurants, specialty shops, and uniquely designed apartments on one side, and artists, street performers, fortune tellers, and more on the other.

1.2 Take in the sights of Los Angeles Phil performs at the Walt Disney Concert Hall

When it first opened to the public on Oct. 22, 2003, Walt Disney Concert Hall had become a Los Angeles landmark. The Los Angeles Philharmonic & the Los Angeles Master Chorale perform at the performance hall, which is situated on Grand Avenue in Downtown L.A. and seats approximately 2,200 people. Walt Disney Concert Hall has gained worldwide critical acclaim and accolades from concertgoers for its spectacular architecture and outstanding sound.

1.3 Visit The Theatre at Ace Hotel and immerse yourself in history

The Ace Hotel in Downtown Los Angeles was erected in 1927 as the United Artists Building on Broadway and 9th Street. C. Howard Crane designed the 13-story structure in the Spanish Gothic style, based on the Segovia Cathedral in Spain. The United Artists Theatre was the main movie theatre for Charlie Chaplin, Douglas Fairbanks, Mary Pickford, and D.W. Griffith's film business, United Artists. Three stories of the structure house the spectacular 1,600-seat movie theatre.

1.4 Enter Orbit with the Endeavour Space Shuttle

The California Science Center, which opened in February 1998 in Exposition Park, has more than 400,000 square feet and features four major display areas: World of Life, Ecosystems, Creative World, and the Space Shuttle Endeavour. The Science Center also sponsors worldwide touring exhibits such as The Science Behind Pixar & includes a seven-story IMAX Theater dedicated to educational programming.

1.5 Visit the Natural History Museum late at night

The Natural History Institution's (NHM) First Fridays program introduces visitors to the museum and a unique type of museum experience. During these after-hours events, contemporary science, culture, and personal experience collide. First Friday's programs include talks and tours, as well as live performances by artists, bands, and DJs. The museum is also available to the public, featuring pop-up performances & surprises throughout its historic halls and galleries.

1.6 Visit Dodger Stadium to see a game

Los Angeles is the Land of Champions, with some of the world's best sporting arenas. Two Olympiads, NCAA finals, three Super Bowls, NBA and WNBA championships, the World Series, the Stanley Cup, the FIFA World Cup, and more have all been held in Los Angeles venues.

1.7 At Grand Central Market, you can eat your way around the world

The busy Grand Central Market (GCM), which has been a Downtown L.A. fixture since 1917, has lately welcomed a new wave of food & drink merchants. GCM was designated one of the top ten new restaurants in the U.S by Bon Appétit in August 2014. China Cafe, Roast To Go, & Tacos Tumbras. Grand Central Market has 11 of the best latest food and drinks options.

1.8 Cross HOLLYWOOD BOWL OFF YOUR TO-DO LIST

There are few things more distinctively Los Angeles than enjoying a summer evening underneath the stars at the Hollywood Bowl, listening to a performance. The Bowl has welcomed everybody from The Beatles and Lady Gaga, Bob Dylan to Prince and Radiohead, and is one of the most well-known outdoor venues in the world. You haven't truly experienced Los Angeles until you've seen a show in the Hollywood Bowl.

1.9 BREAK ROOM 86: Sing Your Heart Away

Break Room 86 is an '80s-themed karaoke establishment situated in the back of The Queue Hotel in Koreatown, and its part of the Houston Hospitality entertainment collection. It's always a good time with cocktail names that sound like your favorite teen idol & a soundtrack that sounds like your favorite mixtape. Either you're there just for the karaoke or the Atari, sing on stage with a live band or reserve a private room for yourself and & your pals.

1.10 Exchange LA: Dance the Night Out

Exchange LA is a stunning Art Deco tower that's been converted for the modern nightclub experience. It's named after the building's historic hosting of the Los Angeles stock exchange on the Spring Street. Exchange is one of the few prominent clubs in L.A. that routinely books trance D.J.s in contrast to house & techno D.J.s.

1.11 Bring a picnic lunch to Eat|See|Hear

The event, which occurs on Saturday nights at several locations ranging from Downtown Los Angeles to Santa Monica, is free and open to the public. Eat|See|Hear has the West Coast's largest outdoor screen and cutting-edge audio. Every showing includes a carefully prepared menu of food trucks and an introductory performance by a new band.

1.12 Attend the Downtown L.A. Art Walk to meet new artists.

The Downtown L.A. Art Walk occurs on the second Thursday of every month, rain or shine, year-round, with fascinating and unusual offers around every corner. Many of the Downtown Art Walk activities occur between 2nd and 9th Streets, in & around the galleries on Spring and Main Streets. Throughout Downtown L.A., several art-related events, activities, openings, and special programming occur during the Art Walk. Thousands of visitors converge on the region to catch up with friends and take in the local experience as the evening advances. The participating galleries are open from 12 p.m. until 10 p.m. Details can be found in the individual gallery listings.

1.13 Jazz at LACMA: Get in the Mood

Over one hundred concerts are presented yearly by the award-winning Department of Music Programs at the Los Angeles County Museum of Art (LACMA), showcasing prominent international and local ensembles in classical, jazz, Latin, and new music programs. Jazz at LACMA has previously featured giants, including Wayne Shorter, Kenny Burrell, John Clayton, Arturo Sandoval, Les McCann, Billy Childs, Cannonball-Coltrane Project, and Ernie Watts, and is one of the museum's most popular events.

1.14 Discover the fabled Sunset Strip.

Sunset Boulevard is among the most recognized streets in Los Angeles, and the iconic Sunset Strip, which extends 1.5 miles from West Hollywood to Beverly Hills, is possibly its most recognized segment. Book a room at the historic Chateau Marmont or a modern hotel such as the Andaz West Hollywood, the Mondrian, or the London West Hollywood. The Whisky a Go-Go, The Roxy, and the

Viper Room are still running great, but newer places like Eveleigh, the Church Key, and BOA Steakhouse draw both tourists and residents. Bar Marmont, Skybar, and the Comedy Store are among the nightlife options.

Chapter 2: Los Angeles Tour

Whether you're a first-time tourist to Los Angeles or a lifelong Angeleno, the City of Angels always has something fresh to offer. There are tours available to help you experience L.A. that serve a wide range of budgets and interests. Read on to learn more about Los Angeles tours, including museum and gastronomy excursions to eco-friendly biking and breathtaking helicopter and boat experiences.

2.1 Tour Hollywood at Warner Bros. Studio

The Warner Bros. Studios VIP Tour provides a unique and intimate look into the workings of Hollywood. An interesting two-hour tour takes groups of 12 people across backlot streets, soundstages, sets, & craft shops. There are no two tours alike. Visitors can take a tour of a popular television show's set, watch Foley artists make audio effects for movies, learn how sets are built, explore millions of props, and much more.

2.2 Universal Studios Hollywood Tour

One of Universal Studios Hollywood's must-see attractions is the renowned Studio Tour. The Studio Tour, narrated by Jimmy Fallon, allows visitors to tour the functioning backlot of a real Hollywood film studio. The tram journey brings passengers past sets from films such as "Psycho," "War of the Worlds," "Jaws," & others, as well as some blazing special effects. The tour also includes the world's largest 3-D experience, filmmaker Peter Jackson's heart-pounding King Kong 360 3-D.

2.3 The Art Muse Los Angeles Tour

Art Muse Los Angeles is a group of art historians, artists, and educators who provide private museum visits in Los Angeles. These art experts and enthusiasts provide talks to small groups of people ranging from beginners to collectors and connoisseurs, customizing their presentations for each type of visitor. Many of L.A.'s main institutions, such as the Getty Center, Norton Simon Museum, Hammer Museum, Los Angeles County Museum of Art, and Museum of Contemporary Art, provide tours through Art Muse. Art Muse also organizes tours of the seasonal art fairs & select contemporary art galleries in Los Angeles. Downtown Los Angeles, the

Wilshire Corridor, Culver City, and Bergamot Station are among the districts where gallery tours are offered.

2.4 Hikes and Bikes Los Angeles

Book a Bikes and Hikes LA trip for an eco-friendly, healthy manner to see Los Angeles. These tours are geared for everyone from avid bikers & hikers to beginners and the casual biker/hiker. "L.A. In a Day," a 32-mile, 5-hour excursion, is the most popular trip. The excursions begin in West Hollywood and travel through opulent Beverly Hills and Bel-Air, as well as L.A.'s world-famous beach towns of Santa Monica, Venice, and Marina Del Rey, as well as the historical movie studios of Culver City. Bikes and Hikes LA, which specializes in individual day trips, also offers group trip alternatives for friends and families, corporate clients, social organizations, incentive travel, and school and university groups.

2.5 Catalin Express

Book a Bikes and Hikes LA trip for an eco-friendly, healthy manner to see Los Angeles. These tours are geared for everyone from avid bikers & hikers to beginners and the casual biker/hiker. "L.A. In a Day," a 32-mile, 5-hour excursion, is the most popular trip. The excursions begin in West Hollywood and travel through wealthy Beverly Hills and Bel-Air and L.A.'s world-famous beach towns of Santa Monica, Venice, and Marina Del

Rey, as well as the historical movie studios of Culver City. Bikes and Hikes LA, specializing in individual day trips, also offers group trip alternatives for friends and families, corporate clients, social organizations, incentive travel, and school and university groups.

2.6 Club Crawl Tour Los Angeles

Hollywood Club Crawl leads you on a nightlife tour of 4 Hollywood clubs every Friday and Saturday, with VIP entrance and no cover charges or lineups. Come by yourself, with a date, or with a group for a great night in Hollywood. At 10 p.m., guests gather at the St. Felix on Cahuenga Boulevard. You'll be introduced to your hosts at check-in, given your Club Crawl wristbands, & directed to the bar for exclusive drink specials. For the full night, pre-sale tickets are $25. Cash tickets are available for $30 at the event check-in desk, but only if the event is not sold out.

2.7 Los Angeles Orbic Air Helicopter Tour

Orbic Air has been one of Southern California's finest helicopter companies for over 20 years, providing Los Angeles helicopter charters, Hollywood helicopter tours, helicopter training, aerial photography, production, and helicopter leasing. Orbic Air is located at Van Nuys Airport, centrally positioned in Los Angeles, with easy access to Hollywood, Malibu, and Santa Monica. L.A.

LIVE, Hollywood and the Pacific coast are among the many helicopter tour destinations, as are landing packages like the Romance Package and the Shoreline Picnic.

2.8 Hollywood/Tourcouch Charter & Tours by Starline Tours

Starline Tours has been providing guests from worldwide with the best of Los Angeles since 1935, when it first introduced the Movie Stars Homes Tour. The Grand City Tour, the LGBT itinerary, and one-hour Hollywood Fun Trips are just a few of the sightseeing tours offered by Starline. There are also private bus charters available.

2.9 Sunset Ranch Hollywood Los Angeles

Get in the saddles with Sunset Ranch Hollywood, the only horse ranch in greater Los Angeles, for a unique tour of Griffith Park. Sunset Ranch offers guided trail rides, boarding, and instruction, among other services and activities. The Hollywood Sign is seen from the one trail ride through Griffith Park. The trip to the top of Griffith Park takes two hours and offers a breathtaking panoramic view of Los Angeles. Lunch Ride, BBQ Ride, Sunset Dinner Ride, and Kids' Party are among the additional ride options available.

Chapter 3: Shop Los Angeles

With its movie-star glamour, wide beaches, and legendary nightlife, Los Angeles attracts visitors. The Los Angeles shopping environment, on the other hand, is just as appealing, with everything from designer apparel to electronics & artisan delicacies.

3.1 Rodeo Drive Los Angeles

A stroll down Rodeo Drive in Beverly Hills is a must; the walkways are lined with some of the world's most luxurious and exclusive stores. Armani, Christian Dior, Coco Chanel, and Gucci are just a few well-known fashion houses with outlets here. You can't afford anything if you have to ask what it really costs. However, gawking at the high-end window displays—or the affluent and famous walking their pedigreed canines or driving Lamborghinis along this famed street—is free of charge.

3.2 Farmers Market Los Angeles

Don't miss a stroll around the Farmers Market's shops and stalls on Fairfax Avenue & West Third Street, where produce, as well as other foodstuffs, seem to be crammed into every available area. (There's even a bakery for dogs!) Movie stars and studio executives may be seen grabbing some quick power breakfast. Walt Disney is said to have sat at a table while designing Disneyland. It may be clogged with tourists by the busload, but it's still a wonderful spot to visit.

3.3 Abbot Kenney Boulevard Los Angeles

Abbot Kinney Boulevard in Venice is the place to go for fashionable, unique treasures like vintage apparel and local art.

3.4 Melrose Avenue Los Angeles

Melrose Avenue is where avant-garde clothes, tacky presents, home décor, and pop art may be found. For antique and designer clothing, go to Wasteland, or for art deco design, go to Thanks for the Memories. On Melrose Avenue, celebrities are common; for the best chance of seeing one, visit a busy Saturday and sit outside one of the coffee shops or eateries.

3.5 Montana Avenue Los Angeles

Montana Avenue in Santa Monica is the place to go for breezy, affluent luxury. Designer apparel and home furnishings abound in unique boutiques and galleries; when you need a break, try a yoga class or visit a spa.

3.6 The Groove Los Angeles

The Grove is an outdoor Los Angeles mall surrounded by a beautifully groomed grassy field with a fountain that moves to music on the hour, and it seems like an imagined small town. Take the free electric trolley, which harkens back to a more opulent past, for a leisurely tour of the businesses. Parking is normally ample, but it might not be easy to find on Friday and Saturday nights.

3.7 Citadel Outlets Los Angeles

Only in Los Angeles will you find a former factory that resembles an Assyrian palace and now is home to Calvin Klein, Levi's, Guess, Converse, and other outlet stores. Check for an information booth at Citadel Outlets and inquire about any special promotions that may be offered.

Chapter 4: Entertainment in Los Angeles

The entertainment options in Los Angeles are limitless. A night out in Los Angeles, on the other hand, does not necessitate hundreds of dollars in bottle service. For less than $20, you can enjoy some of L.A.'s most exciting entertainment & nightlife.

4.1 Mayan Theatre Los Angeles

On Friday nights, the Mayan plays a hip-hop, mix of salsa, and house music for a $12 cover charge for all night, or you may sign up for the mayan guest list via their website & get in for free before 10:30 p.m.

4.2 Casey's Irish Pub Los Angeles

On Sunday and Monday nights, Casey's Irish Pub offers all-day happy hour with PBR and pub fries.

4.3 TCL Chinese Theatre IMAX Los Angeles

The legendary TCL Chinese Theatre is the best venue to view a movie in Los Angeles and don't be hesitant with putting your feet and hands in the cement outside.

4.4 The Airliner Los Angeles

Low-End Theory, the famed monthly electronic music showcase that just concluded its 12-year run & launched the careers of musicians like Nosaj Thing and Flying Lotus was held at The Airliner and is still one of L.A.'s best-kept secrets.

4.5 The Satellite Los Angeles

The Satellite is the spot to go if you're looking for up & coming indie bands. Play a game of pool in their back room if you're not enjoying the band on stage.

4.6 The Roxy Los Angeles

There's no better spot to hear raw, unadulterated rock-and-roll than West Hollywood's Sunset Strip. Whenever you visit the Roxy, you won't have to break the bank to have a good time. On the Roxy, the small upstairs bar features a range of intimate concerts for less than $10.

4.7 The Pub at the Golden Road Los Angeles

Beer does not seem to be nasty just because it's cheap. With 20 rotating taps, the Pub at Golden Road Brewing is the place to go for artisan beer. Do Munch on their house made vegan Bavarian pretzel after a pint or two.

4.8 Universal City Walk-Howl at the Moon Los Angeles

Visit Howl at the Moon, a dueling piano bar on Universal City Walk, for a night out. Enjoy three drinks only for the price of one on Sundays.

4.9 McCabe's Guitar Shop Los Angeles

McCabe's Guitar Shop in Santa Monica offers live music in a unique setting. The majority of concerts are under $20.

4.10 The Ice House Los Angeles

Every Thursday at The Ice House in Pasadena, there is a show called Stand Up All-Stars, which features up-and-comers as well as local stalwarts like Adam Carolla. General Admission tickets are $15, while VIP tickets are $20 and feature front-of-line access and preferred seats.

4.11 Bigfoot West Los Angeles

You don't really have to be the next Mariah Carey to have a good time at Bigfoot West's karaoke night. This

Westside favorite has a distinctive atmosphere because of the log cabin atmosphere.

Chapter 5: Eating in Los Angeles

Whether you like to rub elbows with the celebrities at cutting-edge eateries or eat West Coast classics at a vintage diner, trendy Los Angeles has you covered. Eating healthily has never been easier; being the epicenter of a health-conscious lifestyle, LA is home to a plethora of juice bars, vegan-friendly eateries, and organic farmers' markets that will satisfy even the most health-conscious diners.

Here is the list of foods that Los Angeles excels at more than anywhere else in the United States, along with only a few local examples to illustrate the point.

5.1 Fries and burger

This would be a sin to visit Los Angeles without sampling a delicious cheeseburger & fries from In-N-Out Burger, the state's cult burger restaurant. If you order your meal "animal style," a famous "secret menu" euphemism for a substantial topping of melted cheese, Thousand Island dressing, and grilled onions, you'll get bonus points.

Places to try: In-N-Out Burger is a must-try (Apple Pan, Capitol Burger, and Pie N' Burger)

5.2 Sushi

It's no surprise that Los Angeles is famed for its wonderful sushi offerings, with an entire section named "Little Tokyo." Many of LA's high-profile celebs frequent Nobu, which is owned by celebrity chef Nobu (you're likely to see a Kardashian), while Sugarfish, a popular local restaurant, is known for traditional high-quality sushi.

Places to try: Try Nobu (903 La Cienega Boulevard) or Sugarfish in the Little Tokyo neighborhood (various locations)

5.3 Hot Dogs

Hot dogs are a North American favorite that is best eaten from the inside of a baseball stadium. The simple hot dog has been elevated to a whole new level in Los Angeles, with fast food places all over the city delivering their own distinct and scrumptious twist on the American classic.

Places to try: Pink's Hot Dogs (709 North La Brea Avenue) is just a vintage roadside stand known for its chili cheese dog, a frankfurter topped with beef chili, melted cheese, and onions.

5.4 Sandwich with a French dip

The delectable sandwich has its origins in Southern California and is said to have been created by accident by restaurant owner Philippe Mathieu in 1918. Meat is placed in a gravy-dipped French bread, topped with cheese, and served with a selection of sides in this mouthwatering dinner.

Places to try: Philippe The Original is a good place to start (1001 North Alameda)

5.5 Mexican cuisine

It's no secret that LA has some of the best Mexican cuisines in the country, whether it's fresh burritos from the taco truck or chargrilled carne asada from a dine-in restaurant.

Places to try: Broken Spanish offers an elegant and sophisticated twist on Mexican cuisine (1050 South Flower Street). El Chato Taco Truck sells inexpensive, delectable street tacos (5300 West Olympic Boulevard).

5.6 Parmigiana chicken

This dish consists of a breaded chicken breast which is coated in a thick tomato sauce and afterward topped with a variety of cheeses such as parmesan, mozzarella, and provolone.

Places to try: Dan Tana's (9071 Santa Monica Boulevard), a cozy eatery that has been serving up a classic rendition on the famous chicken parm since 1964.

5.7 Toast with Ricotta

Sqirl's ricotta toast has gone viral on Instagram and has become an online legend. People queue outside this unusual cafe to try their thickly sliced brioche toast smeared in homemade ricotta & topped with a variety of colorful jams - a truly delectable way to start the day.

Places to try: Sqirl (720 Virgil Avenue #4) is a good place to start.

5.8 Apple Pie

Dessert lovers need not fear in Los Angeles, which is recognized for its abundance of healthful cafes. The city has some of the greatest spots to try this traditional American delicacy, with many old-school diners & modern pie shops.

Places to try: Jones Hollywood (7205 California State Route 2) is known for having the best apple pie in town.

Since 1947, The Apple Pan (10801 West Pico Boulevard) has served the meal at its typical diner counter.

5.9 Wine

California's official drink is wine, and the state produces some of the best in the world. If you don't want to drive all the way to the vineyards of Napa Valley or the Orange County, you may taste the delectable drink at one of LA's lovely wineries.

Places to try: Malibu Wine Safari (32111 Mulholland Highway) offers scenic views, local wine tastings, or travel downtown for sampling at San Antonio Winery (737 Lamar Street).

Chapter 6: Stay in Los Angeles

Los Angeles is a whirlwind of roads, sleazy suburbs, coastline, high-gloss neighborhoods, & the extreme lifestyles, all surrounded by the sandy beaches & snowcapped mountains soaring above 10,000 feet. Because the region you choose to stay in could have a massive effect on the trip, we've put together a list of the best places to stay within Los Angeles.

6.1 Places to stay in Downtown

Downtown Los Angeles, the city's historic hub, has undergone a revival. Apartments have been converted from elegant historical banks and the hotels. LA Live, a $2.5 billion of shopping & entertainment complex, has brought the cinemas, high-end hotels, a variety of restaurants, and nightclubs to the area.

However, it is still a diverse neighborhood, with adobe structures & skid row (one of the greatest concentrations of the homeless persons in the United States), Mexican market stalls, avant-garde art galleries, & high-rise of corporate towers all within a few blocks.

There is a wide range of accommodations available, from simple beds to opulent hotels. However, though Downtown is a center of the MTA's networks & public transportation, getting to the beaches isn't easy.

1. **Ace Hotel is the best place to stay in Los Angeles if you want a cool Los Angeles style:** This modern hotel in the middle of Downtown provides clean, trendy rooms and the rooftop pool.

2. **Los Angeles Athletics Club is a sports club based in Los Angeles:** The top 3 floors of the private clubhouse a hotel with around 72 tastefully decorated rooms; the real advantage is a complimentary access to the club's gym, whirlpool, & sauna.

6.2 Places to Stay in the Hollywood

Hollywood has lured millions of visitors, and the equal number of the hopefuls enticed by the potential of riches & glory since movies & their stars emerged international emblems of the good life.

With the creation of the new tourist plaza & shopping malls in recent years, things have lightened up. Today, corporate hype, Hollywood's contradictory elements of freshly polished nostalgia, & deep set seediness make it one of LA's most diverse neighborhoods – and among the greatest sites for the bar-hopping & clubbing.

1. **Hollywood Bed and Breakfast is the best place to stay for a unique experience.** This B & B is housed in 1912 mansion that seems like it belongs from Dr Seuss book. With 4 cozy rooms & a little pool, it's close to everything.

2. **Magic Castle Hotel is the best choice for the modern simplicity.** A popular hotel featuring clean, modern rooms & suites, as well as a heated pool & free drink, sweets, and cookies available 24 hours in a day.

6.3 Places to Stay in West LA

The so-called "Westside" of Los Angeles begins just beyond Hollywood in West LA, home to some of the city's most affluent neighborhoods.

The restaurants & boutiques of West Hollywood & Beverly Hills and the magnificent Getty Center, perched high above the Los Angeles basin, are highlights.

1. **Farmer's Daughter is the best for Midwestern kitsch:** This attractive boutique establishment with aspects of "country fashioned" Midwestern kitsch is located right next to (naturally) the Farmers' Market.

2. **Bel-Air is the best place to go for unfettered luxury:** Constructed in 1946 and now managed by the Sultan of Brunei, LA's most opulent hotel is set in a lushly vegetated canyon and designed as an Arabian oasis.

3. **Beverly Hills is the best place for celebrity-like living:** This luxurious hotel on Sunset Boulevard, dubbed "The Pink Palace," has a full-service La Prairie Spa as well as a lovely outdoor pool.

6.4 Places to Stay in Santa Monica, Malibu & Venice

1. **Ambrose is the best option for a beach bed:** With Arts & Crafts-style decor & boutique accommodations, this is the greatest option for inland Santa Monica.

2. **Channel Road Inn is ideal for a romantic break:** The B&B rooms here are set in lower Santa Monica Canyon (northwest of Santa Monica) and provide beach views, a hot tub, and complimentary bike rentals.

3. **The Kinney is the best place to visit in Venice Beach:** This stylish California hotel is just 0.9 miles from Venice Beach and features bicycle rentals, an outside area with such a fire pit, an outdoor heated pool, and ping pong tables.

6.5 Places to Stay in South Bay

1. **The Beach House is the best place to stay if you want to be pampered to the max**: Fireplaces, balconies, wet bars, hot tubs, stereos, and refrigerators are all available in the two-room suites. Many of the accommodations have views of the ocean.

2. **Portofino Hotel & Yacht Club has the best views of the sea:** The top suites of this oceanfront suite hotel include hot tubs and beautiful views of King Harbor's affluent playground.

6.6 Places to Stay in Orange country

1. **Huntington Surf Inn is the best place to stay in town if you want to go surfing**: With nine modest but incredibly cool rooms with a pop-art decor centered on Southern California beach & surfing culture, the hotel is right on the beach and near to the pier. Many professional surfers choose to reside here.

2. **The Ritz-Carlton Laguna Niguel is the best place to stay if you want to be near the water**: This beautiful Ritz-Carlton is possibly the best in town due to its gorgeous oceanfront location. The rooms and suites are lavishly appointed.

Los Angeles Map

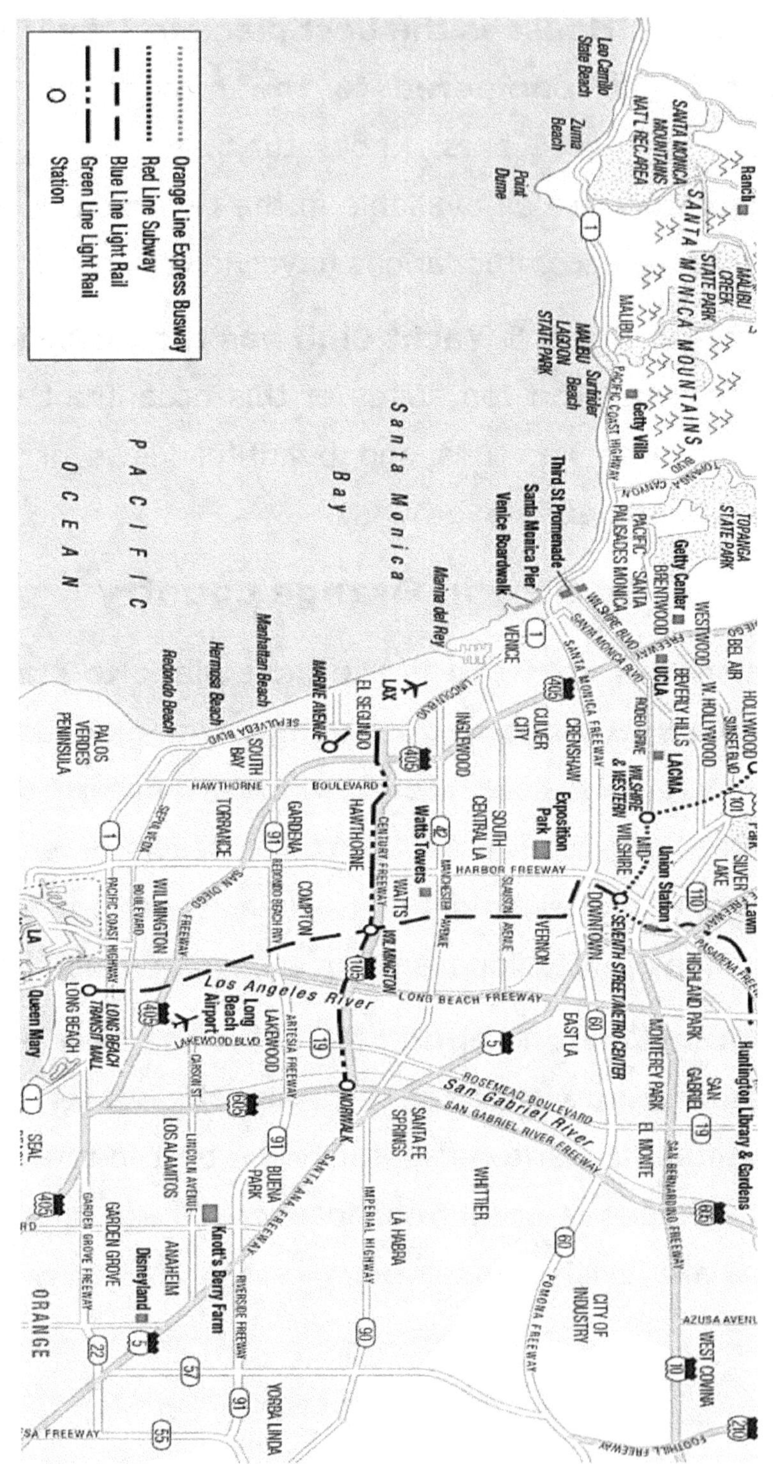